CODE, CONFLICT, CREATURES

THE QUANTUM REVOLUTION AND THE MIDDLE EAST

Ellea Blake

CODE, CONFLICT, CREATURES

CODE, CONFLICT, CREATURES

The Quantum Revolution and the Middle East

Ellea Blake

CONTENTS

Quantum computers promise to revolutionize industries from drug discovery to finance, but also threaten current encryption methods. Researchers are racing to develop quantum-resistant encryption to stay ahead of cyber threats. Startups and big tech are in a heated race to build the first robust quantum computer, with governments driving innovation. The future of quantum tech is bright, filled with transformative applications and profound philosophical questions. □□□□

At COP27, protesters demanded immediate climate action while leaders debated tech solutions. Techno-optimists like Eric Toon of Breakthrough Energy believe in innovations like direct air carbon capture and nuclear fusion, but critics like Mark Jacobson argue these are distractions and greenwashing. Jacobson advocates for existing renewable technologies, while Toon sees a role for both old and new tech. The challenge is immense, but the race to find solutions is on. □□□□

Elon Musk's chaotic takeover of Twitter has sparked debate about the future of social media. While platforms like Facebook struggle to attract new users,

TikTok's rise highlights a shift towards entertainment. The creator economy is booming, with content creators becoming powerful influencers. However, the relationship between creators and platforms is at an inflection point, with creators seeking more independence and fair pay. The future of social media is uncertain but filled with opportunities for innovation and community-focused networks. ▢▢▢▢

In Israel, scientist Yossi Oval ventures into a bat cave near Tel Aviv to study bat vocalizations using AI. Despite the challenging conditions, Yossi's research reveals that bats communicate in complex ways, similar to humans. His work highlights the potential of AI to decode animal communication, offering insights into the natural world. Although limitations exist, Yossi's dedication drives the pursuit of understanding these fascinating creatures. ▢▢▢

PART II

The U.S. faces a complex geopolitical landscape with China and Russia as major powers. General Mark Milley plays a pivotal role in managing this dynamic, particularly in the Ukraine conflict. The path to a negotiated settlement is challenging, with Russia's objectives evolving and Ukraine's military capabilities improving. The U.S. must prevent a China-Russia alliance and maintain a strong military to deter conflict. Technological advancements are changing the character of war, making future conflicts more lethal and unpredictable. Alliances and diplomacy are crucial in this new world order to prevent great power wars and maintain global security. ▢▢▢

The Middle East's stability is precarious, with underlying conflicts, authoritarian regimes, and the Israeli-Palestinian issue posing significant challenges. The U.S. sought to reduce its role, prioritizing other global challenges like China, but misjudgments in its exit strategy have exacerbated regional tensions. Iran's influence, Hamas's actions, and the risk of escalation highlight the need for a reassessment of U.S. policy. Addressing the Palestinian issue, curbing authoritarianism, and managing regional powers are crucial for a more stable and secure Middle East. ▢▢▢

PREFACE

Welcome to the 21st century—a time of mind-blowing tech advancements and some seriously complex geopolitics. As you flip through these pages, you're standing at a crossroads where the world is both thrilling and daunting. "Code, Conflict, Creatures: The Quantum Revolution and the Middle East" is your guide through this maze of change, giving you the insights and understanding you need to navigate our interconnected world with confidence.

In the following pages, we're going on a journey that dives into the profound implications of the quantum revolution, the intricate dynamics of the Middle East, and the interplay between technology and society. This book isn't just a bunch of facts and figures; it's a lens that lets you see the hidden patterns and tangled webs shaping our reality.

The Quantum Revolution

The quantum revolution is more than just a scientific breakthrough; it's a paradigm shift redefining what's possible. From quantum computing to artificial intelligence, the tech landscape is evolving at a breathtaking pace. But with great power comes great responsibility. As we harness the potential of these new technologies, we also have to grapple with the ethical, social, and political challenges they present.

In this book, we'll delve into the world of AI, looking at its impact on everything from healthcare to national security. We'll explore how social media shapes public opinion and how technology is reshaping our relationships with each other and the natural world. Through engaging narratives and real-world examples, you'll gain a deep understanding of the forces driving the quantum revolution and the opportunities and challenges it presents.

The Middle East: A Crucible Of Conflict And Change

The Middle East is a region of stark contrasts and complex dynamics. It's a place where ancient traditions coexist with cutting-edge technology, where political tensions simmer beneath the surface, and where the actions of a few can have global repercussions. Understanding the Middle East is essential for anyone seeking to make sense of the modern world.

In "Code, Conflict, Creatures," we'll examine the historical, cultural, and political forces shaping the Middle East. We'll explore the role of technology in the region, from the use of social media in political uprisings to the impact of AI on military strategies. Through the lens of the Middle East, you'll gain a deeper appreciation of the interconnectedness of our world and the ways in which local conflicts can have global implications.

The Interconnectedness Of Humans And Animals

In an era of rapid technological change, it's easy to lose sight of the natural world and our place within it. But as we explore the interconnectedness of humans and animals, we're reminded of the profound ways our lives are intertwined. From the use of AI in wildlife conservation to the ethical dilemmas posed by animal-machine hybrids, the relationship between humans and animals is being transformed by technology.

In this book, we'll examine how technology is reshaping our understanding of the natural world and our place within it. We'll explore the ethical, social, and political implications of these changes and consider the role that technology can play in promoting a more sustainable and harmonious future.

Navigating A Tripolar World Order

As the 21st century unfolds, the world is becoming increasingly polarized. The rise of new global powers and the shifting dynamics of international relations are reshaping the geopolitical landscape. Understanding this tripolar world order is essential for anyone seeking to navigate the complexities of the modern world.

In "Code, Conflict, Creatures," we'll examine the forces driving the tripolar world order and the implications for global stability and security. We'll explore the role of technology in shaping international relations and consider the ways in which the quantum revolution is reshaping the balance of power. Through engaging narratives and real-world examples, you'll gain a deep understanding of the challenges and opportunities presented by a tripolar world order.

Your Roadmap To The 21St Century

This book is more than just a collection of facts and figures; it's a roadmap to the 21st century. It's a guide that will help you make sense of the complexities of our interconnected world and navigate the challenges and opportunities that lie ahead. Whether you're a student, a professional, or simply a curious observer, "Code, Conflict, Creatures" will provide you with the insights and understanding you need to thrive in the modern world.

So, let's embark on this journey together. Let's explore the mysteries of the quantum revolution, the complexities of the Middle East, and the interconnectedness of humans and animals. Let's navigate the challenges and opportunities of a tripolar world order and gain a deeper understanding of the forces shaping our future.

A NOTE TO THE READER

As I sit down to pen this note, I am filled with a sense of excitement and anticipation. The journey you are about to embark on in "Code, Conflict, Creatures: The Quantum Revolution and the Middle East" is one that has been years in the making, a labor of love and curiosity that has taken me across continents and through the intricate webs of technology, politics, and nature.

In writing this book, my goal was to create a comprehensive guide that would help you navigate the complexities of our interconnected world. We live in an era of rapid change, where the boundaries between the digital and the physical, the local and the global, are blurring at an unprecedented pace. Understanding these shifts is not just an intellectual exercise; it is a necessity for anyone seeking to make sense of the modern world and their place within it.

Throughout these pages, you will explore the quantum revolution and its profound implications for our future. You will delve into the intricate dynamics of the Middle East, a region that is both a crucible of conflict and a beacon of change. You will examine the interconnectedness of humans and animals, and the ways in which technology is reshaping our understanding of the natural world. And you will gain a deeper appreciation of the tripolar world order that is emerging, and the challenges and opportunities it presents.

As you read, I encourage you to approach each chapter with an open mind and a curious heart. Engage with the ideas, question the assumptions, and reflect on how they resonate with your own experiences and beliefs. This book is not a definitive answer to the questions of our time; rather, it is a starting point for a conversation, a spark that I hope will ignite your own journey of discovery.

With heartfelt gratitude and excitement for the journey ahead,

Ellea Blake

PART I

⬚ Quantum Revolution: Unlocking the Future! ⬚

Ever heard of quantum computers? They're not just sci-fi anymore. Imagine a machine that can crack passwords in seconds and revolutionize industries like drug development and finance. Intrigued? Keep reading!

Quantum computers use qubits that can exist in multiple states at once, thanks to quantum mechanics. This allows them to process information exponentially faster than traditional computers. We're talking about groundbreaking scientific discoveries and AI breakthroughs. Mind-blowing, right?

But hold on, there's a catch. While quantum computers have immense potential, they also pose a cybersecurity threat. They could potentially break current encryption standards, putting sensitive data at risk. So, how do we protect against this quantum menace? Let's dive into proactive measures and quantum-resistant encryption.

Now, let's talk about the real heroes behind this quantum revolution – the quantum engineers! They're working tirelessly to build these mind-bending machines in massive, fridge-sized cylinders. It's like a sci-fi movie coming to life in California's Santa Barbara. Get ready to be amazed by the challenges and future prospects of quantum engineering.

And here's the kicker – quantum technology extends beyond computing. Quantum sensors are opening up a whole new frontier with applications that could reshape our world. From drug discovery to climate change solutions, the potential is mind-boggling. The future of quantum is bright, and it's not just about computers. Exciting, isn't it?

QUANTUM REVOLUTION

The Challenge Of Password Cracking

Imagine a machine capable of performing calculations that would take a traditional computer billions of years. This isn't science fiction; it's the promise of quantum computers. These groundbreaking devices, operating on the principles of quantum physics, have the potential to revolutionize industries from finance to pharmaceuticals.

To understand the power of quantum computers, let's consider a simple task: cracking passwords. While traditional computers must methodically try every possible combination, quantum computers can explore multiple possibilities simultaneously. This parallel processing ability allows them to solve complex problems, such as password cracking, exponentially faster.

Traditional password cracking involves brute-forcing through countless combinations, a process that can take years, even for powerful computers. However, passwords based on random characters present a significantly greater challenge. The sheer number of possible combinations makes them virtually unbreakable for classical computers.

Quantum computers, equipped with qubits (quantum bits) that can exist in multiple states simultaneously, can efficiently tackle this problem. By leveraging the principles of superposition and entanglement, they can explore all possible password combinations simultaneously, dramatically reducing the time required to find the correct solution.

The implications of quantum computing extend far beyond password cracking. These powerful machines could:

1. Accelerate drug discovery: By simulating molecular interactions at a quantum level, researchers can identify potential drug candidates more efficiently.
2. Optimize financial modeling: Quantum algorithms can process vast datasets to make more accurate predictions and optimize investment strategies.
3. Address climate change: Quantum computers could help develop new materials for energy storage and devise more efficient solutions for climate mitigation.

4. Enhance artificial intelligence: By enabling more complex machine learning models, quantum computing could lead to significant advancements in AI.

While the potential benefits of quantum computing are immense, it's crucial to acknowledge the potential risks. The same quantum algorithms that can revolutionize industries can also be used to break current encryption standards, compromising the security of sensitive data.

The quantum computing revolution is on the horizon. As researchers continue to develop more powerful quantum machines, we can expect to see transformative advancements across various fields. However, it is imperative to address the security challenges posed by this technology to ensure a responsible and beneficial future.

Quantum Computing And The Cybersecurity Threat

Quantum computers, while still in their infancy, hold the potential to revolutionize computing. However, they also pose a significant threat to current encryption standards. This article explores the potential impact of quantum computers on cybersecurity, the challenges of developing quantum-resistant encryption, and the urgent need for proactive measures to protect against future threats.

Quantum computers, unlike classical computers that process information in bits, utilize qubits. These qubits can exist in multiple states simultaneously, allowing quantum computers to perform certain calculations exponentially faster. One such calculation is factoring large numbers, a process that underpins many modern encryption algorithms, including RSA.

The RSA encryption algorithm is based on the difficulty of factoring large numbers into their prime factors. While classical computers struggle with this task, quantum computers, using Shor's algorithm, can potentially factor these numbers efficiently. This could render RSA and other public-key cryptographic systems vulnerable to attack.

The Race To Quantum-Resistant Encryption

To counter the threat posed by quantum computers, researchers are working on developing quantum-resistant encryption algorithms. These algorithms are designed to be secure even against attacks from powerful quantum computers.

Creating quantum-resistant encryption algorithms is a complex task. These algorithms must be mathematically sound, computationally efficient, and capable of withstanding various attacks. Additionally, they must be compatible with existing cryptographic infrastructure.

The Nist Post-Quantum Cryptography Standardization Process

To address the urgency of this issue, the National Institute of Standards and Technology (NIST) launched a competition to identify promising quantum-resistant encryption algorithms. After a rigorous evaluation process, NIST selected four algorithms as finalists for standardization.

While the development of quantum-resistant encryption is underway, it is essential to take proactive measures to protect against potential quantum attacks. This includes:

1. Harvesting and Storing Data: Malicious actors may be collecting encrypted data today with the intention of decrypting it using future quantum computers.
2. Updating Encryption Standards: Organizations should transition to quantum-resistant encryption algorithms as soon as they become standardized.

3. Raising Awareness: Educating individuals and organizations about the quantum threat is crucial for fostering a proactive approach to cybersecurity.

The advent of quantum computers presents a significant challenge to cybersecurity. While the development of quantum-resistant encryption is progressing, it is imperative to adopt a proactive stance to protect against potential threats. By understanding the risks and taking appropriate measures, we can mitigate the impact of quantum computing on cybersecurity and ensure a secure digital future.

Quantum Engineering: A Revolution In The Making

In the heart of California's Santa Barbara, a revolution is brewing. Engineers are working tirelessly to develop quantum computers, machines capable of solving problems that would stump even the most powerful classical computers.

Eric Lucero, a quantum engineer at Google, is at the forefront of this technological revolution. His team is building quantum computers, housed in massive, fridge-sized cylinders. These machines utilize delicate, gold-plated structures that harness the mysterious properties of quantum physics.

Quantum computers are poised to transform industries such as drug development and logistics. Their ability to solve complex mathematical problems could lead to groundbreaking scientific discoveries and even help model the universe.

Companies like Google, IBM, and Microsoft are investing heavily in quantum computing research. While the potential applications are vast, the immediate focus is on scaling up these machines to achieve the necessary processing power.

The Challenges Of Scaling Quantum Computers

One of the biggest challenges in quantum computing is scaling up the number of qubits. These quantum bits are extremely sensitive and require precise control to maintain their quantum states. Factors like heat, electrical signals, and even cosmic rays can disrupt qubits, leading to errors in calculations.

Tech companies are competing to build the first quantum computer capable of achieving quantum supremacy, a point at which it can perform tasks that classical computers cannot. However, this goal remains elusive, with current prototypes still falling short of the necessary qubit count.

Despite the excitement surrounding quantum computing, it's essential to maintain a realistic perspective. While the potential applications are promising, the challenges of building scalable and reliable quantum computers are significant.

Quantum computing represents a groundbreaking technological advancement with the potential to revolutionize various industries. However, the road to realizing this potential is fraught with challenges. As researchers continue to push the boundaries of quantum engineering, the future of computing remains uncertain, but filled with promise.

Quantum computers harness the power of quantum mechanics to perform calculations that would be impossible for traditional computers. These machines operate in a realm where particles can exist in multiple states simultaneously and become entangled, defying the laws of classical physics.

The Quantum World

The Power Of Qubits

The foundation of quantum computers lies in quantum mechanics, a theory that describes the behavior of subatomic particles. Unlike classical mechanics, quantum mechanics introduces concepts such as superposition and entanglement. Superposition allows particles to exist in multiple states at once, while entanglement links particles across vast distances. Quantum computers use qubits, the quantum equivalent of classical bits. Unlike bits, which can only be 0 or 1, qubits can exist in a superposition of both states. This allows quantum computers to process information exponentially faster than classical computers.

Entanglement is another key concept in quantum computing. When qubits are entangled, they become interconnected, regardless of distance. This allows for parallel processing and the ability to explore multiple possibilities simultaneously.

Quantum computers have the potential to revolutionize various fields, including:

1. Drug discovery: Simulating molecular interactions at a quantum level can accelerate the development of new drugs.
2. Materials science: Quantum computers can help design new materials with enhanced properties.
3. Optimization problems: Complex optimization problems, such as traffic management or financial modeling, can be solved more efficiently.
4. Artificial intelligence: Quantum computing can enhance machine learning algorithms and lead to breakthroughs in AI.

Challenges And Future Prospects

Despite their immense potential, quantum computers face

significant challenges. Maintaining the delicate quantum states of qubits and scaling up these machines to a practical size are major hurdles. However, researchers are making progress in addressing these challenges.

As quantum computing technology continues to advance, we can expect to see transformative applications that were previously unimaginable. The future of quantum computers is bright, with the potential to reshape our world in profound ways.

Quantum Sensors: A New Frontier

While quantum computers garner much attention, quantum technology extends far beyond the realm of computing. Quantum sensors, utilizing the principles of quantum mechanics, offer a wide range of applications with profound implications for various fields.

Quantum Brain Scanning

Quantum brain scanners, a recent development, have revolutionized the study of brain activity, particularly in young children. These scanners, equipped with quantum sensors, provide unprecedented clarity and accuracy in capturing brain signals. They are less intrusive and allow participants to move freely, making them ideal for studying the brains of children who struggle to remain still.

Quantum sensors have diverse applications beyond brain scanning:

1. Navigation: Improved navigation systems based on Earth's magnetic field.
2. Environmental Monitoring: Detecting subtle changes in gravity for underground monitoring and climate change studies.

3. Infrastructure Monitoring: Assessing the stability of large structures like railroads.
4. Medical Research: Studying brain activity in patients with neurological conditions like Parkinson's disease.

Quantum sensors offer unprecedented levels of precision and sensitivity, enabling us to gather valuable information about our world. They have the potential to revolutionize industries such as:

1. Geology: Understanding the Earth's structure and dynamics.
2. Environmental Science: Monitoring climate change and natural resources.
3. Infrastructure: Ensuring the safety and efficiency of large structures.
4. Medicine: Advancing medical research and diagnosis.

The Future Of Quantum Technology

Quantum technology, encompassing both quantum computers and quantum sensors, holds immense promise. As these technologies continue to evolve, we can expect to see groundbreaking advancements across various fields. The future of quantum technology is bright, and its potential impact on society is immeasurable.

In our ongoing exploration of quantum technology, we've seen how the subatomic realm defies our conventional understanding of reality. Today, we delve into one of the most astounding and confounding examples of quantum technology: quantum entanglement and teleportation.

In the early 2000s, a group of Austrian scientists, led by physicist Anton Zeilinger, conducted a groundbreaking experiment on the banks of the Danube River in Vienna. Their goal? To teleport a photon using the mysterious phenomenon of quantum entanglement. In this process, one of the entangled photons remained with the sender, while the other was transmitted across the river. Quantum entanglement created an inexplicable connection between the two particles, enabling the transfer of information and, ultimately, the teleportation of the photon's quantum state.

This remarkable feat, known as quantum teleportation, has since been achieved over even greater distances, such as the 150-kilometer span between the islands of La Palma and Tenerife. Chinese researchers have even successfully teleported quantum states from a ground station to a satellite. These advancements in quantum teleportation exemplify our growing understanding of quantum physics and pave the way for the development of new quantum technologies.

One such technology is the quantum internet, which would use quantum teleportation to transmit data between quantum computers with exceptional security and power. By connecting quantum computers, a quantum internet could revolutionize data transfer, surpassing the traditional binary code of classical computers. However, Anton Zeilinger suggests that the potential applications of quantum teleportation extend far beyond a new internet. In the future, teleporting larger objects and even living organisms could become a reality, despite the current challenges.

To better understand the philosophical implications and profound questions raised by quantum technology, we turn to David Deutsch, a pioneer in the field of quantum computing and professor at Oxford University. Deutsch's groundbreaking work in the 1980s built upon Alan Turing's concept of a universal machine, incorporating the principles of quantum physics to propose the idea of a quantum computer. These theoretical devices, operating on the laws of quantum physics, could perform computations far beyond the capabilities of classical computers.

Deutsch's insights have sparked a race among tech companies to develop quantum computers. However, his current focus lies in exploring what these powerful machines can reveal about the fundamental nature of our universe. Quantum computers, according to Deutsch, defy conventional rules of computation and suggest that the true nature of reality extends far beyond our current perceptions. To explain the extraordinary capabilities of quantum computers, Deutsch invokes the many-worlds interpretation of quantum mechanics.

The many-worlds interpretation, first introduced in the 1950s, posits that random events give rise to numerous versions of reality. In this view, quantum computers access multiple parallel realities to perform their seemingly impossible calculations. Although this interpretation may seem unconventional, Deutsch argues that it is a logical outcome of quantum mechanics and is supported by many working on quantum computers.

However, not all physicists agree with the many-worlds interpretation. Carlo Rovelli, a prominent figure in the field, has previously criticized the idea as "crazy," acknowledging that any attempt to comprehend quantum mechanics challenges our conventional understanding of the world. Rovelli emphasizes that the reality described by quantum mechanics is vastly different from our everyday experiences, a divergence that became apparent in the early days of quantum mechanics nearly a century ago.

As we continue to explore the peculiarities of quantum technology and their implications for our understanding of reality, it is essential to consider the philosophical questions they raise. The world of the subatomic is indeed a bewildering place, but it is through our ongoing efforts to unravel its mysteries that we can hope to unlock the true potential of quantum technology.

The Interconnected Reality

Quantum mechanics challenges our intuitive understanding of the world, revealing that nothing exists independently. Reality is not composed of individual objects but rather the connections between them. According to this view, particles, galaxies, and even stones do not possess inherent positions or properties. Instead, properties emerge from the interactions and relationships between different elements of nature. To truly understand nature, we must consider these interdependencies and the web of connections that bind the universe together.

This interconnected view of reality may seem counterintuitive, but it is at the heart of quantum mechanics. It suggests that objective reality, as we commonly perceive it, may not exist. Instead, the world consists of relationships between objects, which give rise to the properties we observe. Whether this notion is more or less bewildering than the many-worlds interpretation is a matter of personal preference, as physicists do not unanimously agree on a single interpretation of quantum mechanics.

One might ask why we should bother contemplating such abstract concepts. After all, our everyday experiences seem unaffected by whether we live in a multiverse or a world of interconnections. However, for those seeking to understand the inner workings of quantum technology, grappling with these profound questions is essential. David Deutsch, a pioneer in quantum computing, believes that addressing these questions can lead to the development of superior technology.

Anton Zeilinger, the Nobel Prize-winning physicist who conducted the groundbreaking quantum teleportation experiment, shares this perspective. For Zeilinger, the true value of quantum technology lies not just in its practical applications but in the fundamental questions it raises about the nature of the universe and our role within it. He hopes that future generations will uncover the true workings of quantum mechanics, revealing the underlying reasons for its existence.

Quantum technology, with its potential to revolutionize computing and our understanding of the universe, is ushering in a new era. As we harness the extraordinary power of quantum computers, we gain the ability to perform tasks previously deemed impossible. But the true fascination of this technology lies in its capacity to provide insights into the nature of reality that no other technology can offer. Quantum computers, with their seemingly radical and otherworldly capabilities, are a reflection of the quantum world in which we live.

The world of quantum technology is as bewildering as it is awe-inspiring. From quantum entanglement and teleportation to the interconnected nature of reality, our exploration of the quantum realm challenges our intuitions and expands our understanding of the universe. As we continue to push the boundaries of quantum technology, we must also engage with the profound philosophical questions it raises.

The pursuit of understanding, driven by curiosity and a desire to uncover the fundamental workings of the universe, is at the heart of scientific inquiry. Quantum technology, with its potential to revolutionize industries and reshape our world, is a testament to the power of human ingenuity and our insatiable quest for knowledge. As we stand on the precipice of a new quantum era, let us embrace the challenges and opportunities that lie ahead, for they hold the key to unlocking the true potential of quantum technology and the secrets of the universe itself.

The Road To Robust Quantum Computers

The quantum computing industry is abuzz with excitement, yet a stark reality lingers: current quantum computers do not perform very well. Most machines operate with around 430 qubits, far short of the estimated 1,000,000 qubits needed for significant breakthroughs. We spoke with industry leaders to discuss the path forward and the opportunities that lie ahead.

Steve Brierley, CEO of River Lane

"Building a large and reliable quantum computer is one of the greatest challenges humanity has undertaken. The ability to harness the properties of atoms will transform our understanding of nature and open up possibilities for new products in industries like healthcare and climate change mitigation. Quantum computers will serve as a tool for designing on a computer, replacing current experimental methods in laboratories."

Brierley draws a parallel with Moore's Law, which demonstrates that consistent improvement over time leads to exponential advancements. He believes that the same progress is occurring in quantum computing. However, two major challenges must be overcome: scaling up the systems and increasing their size.

Elana Whisby, CEO of Oxford Quantum Circuits

Whisby emphasizes the need to escalate our capacity from 100 to 1000 qubits and eventually to millions. Additionally, enhancing the dependability of the system, its components, and the error correction process during computer operation is crucial. She highlights the importance of processing the vast amounts of data generated by quantum computers in real-time to rectify errors during computation.

The Promise Of Quantum Technology

Despite the current limitations, quantum technology already shows promise in various applications. Brierley mentions that customers are already using their systems for optimization problems, molecular simulations, battery development, pharmaceutical research, risk optimization in finance, creative portfolio analysis, and automotive simulations.

According to a collaborative paper by Jay Gambetta from IBM and other US universities, we can expect to see quantum advantage within the next 3 to 5 years. The transition to quantum computing will have a significant impact on businesses, with the future quantum realm seamlessly integrating with existing technologies.

Investing In Quantum Computing

Herman Hauser, Investor in Quantum Technology

Hauser draws comparisons between the growth of classical computing and the current state of quantum computing. He believes that the interfaces in quantum computing have not yet solidified, making it an exciting time for investment. He has invested in both hardware and software companies, highlighting the unique approach of ParityQC, which focuses on efficient parity spaces for significant advantages in parallelization.

The Hybrid Model Of Quantum And Classical Computers

Steve Brierley

Brierley elaborates on the current use cases for the hybrid model of quantum and classical computers. Quantum computing is always considered hybrid, as certain parts of a problem are better suited for quantum computers, while others are more suitable for classical computers. He mentions methods like embedding, which involve modeling a system at different length scales.

Elana Whisby

Whisby shares her initiatives at Oxford Quantum Circuits, emphasizing the importance of seamless interchangeability between CPUs and QPUs (quantum processing units) with super low latency. She highlights their next-generation systems, like Tashiko in Tokyo and the upcoming Shihiko, which will allow customers to easily add a QPU to their existing services.

The Quantum Race: Startups Vs. Big Tech

The panel discusses whether startups or big tech companies will emerge as frontrunners in the quantum race. Hauser believes the race is wide open, with numerous technologies vying for the top spot. Brierley argues that every major technological shift has given rise to companies like Google, Arm, and Qualcomm, which were all startups at one point. He is confident in the immense positive impact that quantum technology can have and believes in the competitive advantage of smaller companies.

The panel agrees that government procurement is crucial for driving innovation and ensuring successful implementation. Hauser emphasizes the importance of governments acting as customers to create market demand. Whisby highlights the UK government's excellent job in this regard, with a combination of government procurement, private investment, and government investment driving the ecosystem forward.

The quantum computing industry stands at a critical juncture. Despite the current limitations, the potential applications and the promise of exponential scaling make it an exciting time for investment and innovation. As governments and private investors drive the ecosystem forward, the future of quantum computing will likely involve a diverse and thriving landscape of startups and big tech companies working together to tackle the challenges ahead. The once-in-a-lifetime opportunity to contribute to the creation of this emerging industry is within reach, and the time to act is now.

Techno-Optimism or Greenwashing? The Battle for Climate Solutions

Ever wondered about the future of renewable energy and climate tech? Let's dive into a fascinating read about the challenges and promises of clean energy solutions. Strap in for a wild ride through the world of renewables and climate change!

COP27 in Sharm el Sheikh saw countries agree on a new fund for climate loss and damage, but tougher steps to reduce fossil fuel use remained elusive. The pressure to address climate change is intense, and billions of dollars are pouring into technologies like green hydrogen and direct air capture. But are they the real deal?

Meet Jacobson, the renewable energy advocate who's living off the grid in California. He's all about solar, batteries, and electric everything. But is relying solely on renewables feasible on a global scale? And what's the deal with intermittent energy sources like wind and sun? Let's find out!

Jacobson believes in the power of interconnected renewable energy grids, but the costs of upgrading infrastructure are no joke. Is renewable energy really the most cost-effective solution? And what about those flashy moonshot technologies like nuclear fusion and direct air capture? Are they just distractions?

Hold onto your hats, folks, because Jacobson isn't holding back! He's calling out greenwashing and the fossil fuel industry's sneaky tactics. Carbon capture, direct air capture, blue hydrogen - are they really just ploys to keep the fossil fuel industry alive? Let's separate fact from fiction in the world of climate tech.

Fusion, anyone? Jacobson isn't sold on it, calling it "vaporware" and pointing out the damage caused by investing in technologies that don't exist. So, what's the lesson from Cleantech 1.0? Strap in for a rollercoaster ride through the world of climate tech and renewable energy. It's a wild, wild world out there!

TECHNO-OPTIMISM
OR GREENWASHING?

The Battle For Climate Solutions

In the bustling halls of COP27, held in the Egyptian resort of Sharm el Sheikh, protesters chanted, "What do we want? Climate justice! When do we want it? Now!" Despite the country's harsh crackdown on dissent, their voices resonated through the conference, demanding immediate action on climate change.

World leaders, business executives, and officials gathered to discuss strategies to cut global carbon emissions. However, the hope for a major breakthrough was dim. Political turmoil around the world had dampened spirits, and expectations were low. Scientists warn that global carbon emissions need to be cut by nearly half in the next eight years and to virtually zero by 2050. The debate at COP27 centered on how to achieve this goal, with a focus on the role of technology.

The Role Of Technology

Investment in new climate technologies, such as direct air carbon capture, nuclear fusion, and sustainable aviation fuels, has been on the rise. But opinions are divided on whether these innovations are necessary or if they are merely a distraction from the real work of cutting carbon emissions.

Eric Toon, Vice President in Charge of Science Technology at Breakthrough Energy, a venture founded by Microsoft co-founder Bill Gates, believes that technology is pivotal. Breakthrough Energy invests in technologies across various industries, aiming to reduce carbon emissions by at least half a gigaton of CO_2 every year. Toon argues that while existing technologies like wind and solar are important, they are not enough to solve the climate crisis alone.

"We're across the board in electricity, transportation, buildings, manufacturing, and agriculture," Toon explained. "In the electricity sector, we've made significant strides, but we need more. We need technologies that can make a real dent in carbon emissions."

Toon emphasizes that Breakthrough Energy is prepared to invest in technology in any industry, as long as it has the potential to significantly reduce carbon emissions. "Usually, what I tell people is half a gigaton," he said. "If you need a spreadsheet to show me how you get to half a gigaton, never mind, right? I'm looking for ones where it's incredibly obvious."

Breakthrough Energy is investing in all the big examples we've talked about in this series: direct air carbon capture, nuclear fusion, green hydrogen, and cleaner fuels for planes. And on top of that, some pretty out-there ideas like lab-based milk, which promises to cut down on the emissions produced by making infant formula from cow's milk.

"It sort of depends on your definition of crazy, right?" Toon said with a laugh. "I mean, we have a couple of young women who discovered that you can culture mammary epithelial cells in a hollow fiber reactor and make milk. Not a soy milk or an almond milk or a milk substitute, but make actual milk because you've got these mammary epithelial cells, which would normally produce milk in a mammal, right, are producing in a hollow fiber reactor."

Breakthrough Energy is working like a typical venture capital firm, investing in tech startups. It's making bets on which climate tech companies have good ideas that will succeed as profitable businesses. Toon and his colleagues not only think that some of these businesses will succeed, but they believe that this kind of tech innovation will have an important role to play in fighting climate change.

The Critics' Perspective

Mark Jacobson, a professor of civil and environmental engineering at Stanford University, is a vocal critic of techno-optimism. He believes that most of our energy needs can be met with existing renewable technologies like wind, solar, and water. Jacobson argues that investing in new climate tech is a waste of time and money, and that it distracts from the urgent need to deploy existing solutions.

"We don't have time to wait for a miracle technology," Jacobson said. "We need to deploy technologies we have today to solve this problem."

Jacobson has become something of a celebrity in the climate policy world. He's using his own home in California to make his case for renewables. "Well, I built a new home and it's all electric," he explained. "There's no gas. I have solar on the roof, batteries in the garage, electric heat pumps for air and water heating and air conditioning, electric induction cooktop stoves. It's very energy efficient. In five and a half years, I've not paid an electricity bill, a gasoline bill or a natural gas bill. I've provided all my own electricity in the annual average from my rooftop solar."

In fact, Jacobson has generated 20% more than he's needed and has sold that extra back to the grid for an average of about $850 per year. However, converting a house to run on nothing but renewables in a rich country like the US is quite different from doing it throughout the world. One of the problems with using only renewable electricity is that renewable energy sources like the wind or the sun are intermittent. It's not always sunny and it's not always windy.

Jacobson argues that there are ways to fix that. "By interconnecting through the transmission grid, both geographically dispersed wind and geographically dispersed solar, the more interconnections you have, the smoother the overall output supply is," he said. "If you can interconnect Eastern US with Western US, you'd rarely have any time where you have no wind or Eastern Europe with Western Europe and Northern Europe and Southern Europe. You generally have a continuous supply of wind and solar."

However, upgrading electricity grids and storage infrastructure requires significant investment. Jacobson believes that, once the costs of these upgrades are taken into account, renewable energy is still the most cost-effective solution.

"We do want to take advantage of existing infrastructure as much as possible," he said. "But in the end, if we go to this massive scale up, we will need more and more. But we've cost it out and other groups have cost it out. In all cases, they are less expensive than current fossil fuel systems."

Jacobson's plan to save the world involves renewable energy, a vast electricity grid, and batteries in every home. It's not glamorous and it's not very flashy. But it means we don't have to worry about harnessing the power of the stars with miracle fusion power or sucking emissions back out of the atmosphere with direct air carbon capture. They simply aren't needed.

But Jacobson goes even further. He says that not only are these moonshot technologies to fight climate change unnecessary, they're actively stopping us from making the transition to a lower carbon economy.

"Take the example of direct air capture," he said. "Let's say you power that direct air capture with renewable electricity like a wind turbine. What if you instead took that wind farm and you used it to replace a coal plant? There, you not only eliminate the CO2 carbon dioxide emissions from the coal plant itself, you eliminate the coal plant infrastructure, you eliminate the mining of the coal, you eliminate the air pollution from the coal. Whereas if you take that same wind farm and all you do is take carbon dioxide out of the air, the air pollution from the coal plant continues. So it's an opportunity cost."

Jacobson argues that promoting this kind of climate tech is really a form of greenwashing. "The biggest problem we're facing, I think, is we have too many competing proposals like from Bill Gates and others who are pushing continuations of fossil fuels under the guise of doing something good," he said. "And this is classic greenwashing. And I'll just name the greenwash technologies. Carbon capture, every form of carbon capture is a greenwash. Direct air capture, that's a greenwash. Blue hydrogen, that's a greenwash. Those three are all designed to keep the fossil fuel industry in business and they're being promoted by the fossil fuel industry because it keeps them alive and allows them to pollute more, kill more people through their air pollution, all of these technologies."

Nuclear fusion doesn't escape Jacobson's criticisms either. "Fusion is vaporware," he said. "I mean, it doesn't exist. There are all sorts of technologies. I mean, it's great. I mean, fusion is, I don't have as many objections with fusion, but the fact is it doesn't exist. And all these energy technologists do this. They all just want more money to invest in these technologies that don't exist. That's damaging our efforts to solve the problem now."

The Lessons Of Cleantech 1.0

The current wave of investment in climate tech is not the first. The first wave, known as Cleantech 1.0, saw billions of dollars invested in technologies that ultimately failed to deliver. Companies like Solyndra, which developed a new solar panel design, went bankrupt, and the sector as a whole suffered significant losses.

Eric Toon acknowledges the failures of Cleantech 1.0 but argues that the current wave is different. He believes that the lessons learned from the past will lead to more successful investments in climate tech. Toon emphasizes that while technology is not as silver bullet, it is an essential part of the solution.

"When we started this in 2017, we were still mostly looking back over our shoulder at the giant smoking crater that was cleantech 1.0," Toon said. "And so the question is, is there a way to invest in this space and make money? And I think by showing the world that there is a way to invest in this space to make money, we attract more money to this space. And that has obviously a huge impact."

Toon argues that climate tech is no longer treated in the same way as other risky investments in tech startups. "There was a very exuberant period of investment where I think that we attempted to just map cleantech onto the tech investing model that was so successful in the last couple of decades of the last century," he said. "If we think about how tech investing really works, I see 50 opportunities, 43 of those I'm pretty sure aren't going to work. The other seven, I don't know. So I'll give them a little bit of time and a little bit of money and see what happens. And that's fine in tech, because a little bit of time is six months or a year and a little bit of money is $500,000. The problem is that when you get to tough tech and cleantech specifically, all of a sudden a little bit of time is five years and a little bit of money is $30 million. And so the idea that I can seed a whole bunch of things and see what happens, that I don't think maps."

Toon believes that the tech he's investing in does have the potential to succeed and make money for investors and help cut emissions. But what about Mark Jacobson's argument that most of this new technology is simply greenwashing?

"Well, I would say a couple of things," Toon said. "I would say first that some of the statements that Professor Jacobson has made are controversial. The second thing I would say is it's a little bit of a false dichotomy. I mean, Professor Jacobson believes that we can use existing technology to generate a lot more zero carbon power. Absolutely. We can install a lot more wind and solar. So sure, you can do all that stuff. Does that solve our problem in and of itself? No, it doesn't, right? Because of these intermittencies with renewable energy, I want firm power. I want my light to come on when I flip my light switch, not the next time the cloud moves out of the way or the next time that the wind blows. I'm not going to say Mark's crazy or Mark's wrong or anything like that. But I do believe that to just say we can deploy existing technologies is an incomplete solution."

Regardless of whether it's new technology or old technology, Toon acknowledges this is going to be difficult. "This is a challenge that you have with all of the technologies that we're talking about, right?" he said. "None of these technologies scale the way that apps or software scale. They are steel in the ground. They are big projects. They require permitting. It is very challenging to build out this infrastructure. That's true for every single aspect. Yes, I mean, the time constraints that we're up against and the challenges of deploying infrastructure at scale are massive challenges that society is going to have to figure out how they want to deal with."

Toon kept coming back to one point, and it's a point heard a lot in this series. The threat of climate change is huge and we need to throw everything at it. And we just don't have to choose between which approach, which technology will work. We need to try to do them all.

"You know, I think you've got to be careful of forcing these false dichotomies and saying it's one or the other," Toon said. "You know, the name of the game here is to not have emissions. In some instances, I suspect that people are going to say, I don't really care about the details. I just want it as cheap as it can possibly be. And so that might be to drill it out of the ground and do post-combustion capture. In other jurisdictions, people may well say,

I don't like that. I don't like the idea of the oil and gas industry continuing to drill things out of the ground. I don't really like the idea of deploying massive amounts of carbon capture. So no, we're not going to do that. And we're going to pay $150 a barrel or whatever for some kind of synthetic fuel that doesn't produce carbon. And so, you know, should we build out solar and wind? Should we build out storage? Should we build out transmission? Should we do all those things? Absolutely, positively, we should. Should we develop new approaches to zero carbon energy? Absolutely, we should. So it's not an either or, it's an all of the above."

COP27 in Sharm el Sheikh ran more than a day over time before delegates finally thrashed out a deal. In a move that had eluded negotiators for nearly 30 years, countries agreed finally to set up a new fund for climate loss and damage. But they failed to agree on tougher steps to reduce use of the fossil fuels causing that damage, which left many people extremely disappointed.

The enormity of the challenge is daunting, and there is so little time to address it that there's an understandable urge to grasp at every possible solution. Techno-optimists always believe that technology is the answer. It's solved so many problems in our lives already and it's changed our world at such rapid speeds. So surely it can also solve one of the biggest problems of all, climate change.

When the series began, there was skepticism about a lot of the promises being made by climate tech proponents. But by the end of the series, there was a minor change of heart. A machine in Iceland was seen sucking carbon dioxide out of clean air and scientists trying to unlock the revolutionary promise of nuclear fusion. Just one kilogram of fusion fuel produces as much energy as 10 million kilograms of fossil fuels. A startup founder was convinced he could build a supersonic jet powered by green aviation fuel. And a mining magnate was trying to make green hydrogen mainstream.

But the trouble with nearly all these technologies is what came to be known as the 1% problem. Last year, green hydrogen only made up about 1% of global hydrogen supplies. Sustainable aviation fuel accounted for less than 1% of global airlines fuel use. Direct air capture is sucking up an even tinier sliver of global carbon emissions. And nuclear fusion is producing no clean energy whatsoever. The point is, we're running out of time. The climate problem is getting worse by the year. So the pressure to address it is much more intense. That's why billions of dollars are going into these technologies, and some of them will undoubtedly scale up much faster than expected.

In the meantime, the big lesson from this series is that it's obvious we need to double down on every bit of green technology that we already have. Tech planet save. Right now, as you read, there are people looking up at the night sky thinking, what if we could just bottle the power of the stars? What if that is the answer to climate change? Something completely new, a power source we haven't yet harnessed. We've always defined ourselves by the ability to overcome the impossible.

Something like the Hollywood sci-fi blockbuster Interstellar, where a spaceship called Endurance uses star power to travel through space. Perhaps we've just forgotten that we are still pioneers, that we've barely begun, and that our greatest accomplishments cannot be behind us. Well, it turns out the tech imagined in that film Interstellar wasn't entirely science fiction, because bottling the power of the stars is exactly the sort of moonshot tech that some people say could get us out of the fossil fuel mess we've created on planet Earth.

It's an energy source called nuclear fusion. Fusion is the reaction that's powering the stars. So fusion's happening out there in space all the time. It's like the ultimate energy source of the universe. Dr. Melanie Windridge is a fusion scientist. Fusion is different to nuclear fission. That's the reaction that powers conventional nuclear power stations today. Fusion is when small particles come together to make bigger ones, and when it happens, it produces a massive amount of energy. It's why stars like the sun produce heat and light.

"So the sun is essentially a big ball of hydrogen," Windridge explained. "Hydrogen comes together to make helium, and that releases a lot of energy. For decades, scientists have been wondering if it's possible to recreate the nuclear fusion happening in the sun here on Earth. Take some hydrogen, force it together until it fuses to make helium, and harvest the energy. It's been enticing scientists since they first figured out what was causing the sun to shine over 100 years ago, because they realized that if we could do this, we'd have a very potent energy source, one that produces no greenhouse gases, produces no long-lived radioactive waste. It's safe, abundant energy. Just one kilogram of fusion fuel produces as much energy as 10 million kilograms of fossil fuels. So it's a very exciting energy source, if we could harness it on Earth."

The people building these machines say they're getting really close to perfecting the technology. So is the dream of nuclear fusion really about to become a reality? And can it solve our climate change problem for good?

☐ The Golden Era of Social Media ☐

Elon Musk's takeover of Twitter has caused quite a stir, with mixed results. The neighborhood around Twitter's headquarters has seen changes, but not all for the better. Musk's actions have led to significant layoffs and a precarious financial situation. What does this mean for the future of social media platforms? Stay tuned for more! #SocialMediaDrama

The history of Twitter is a fascinating tale of ups and downs. Despite its popularity, Twitter has struggled to turn a profit. Musk's supporters hoped he could turn the company around, but his actions have raised questions about the platform's financial future. Is this the end of an era for Twitter? Let's find out! #TwitterHistory

The creator economy is booming, with content creators gaining more power and influence. Platforms like YouTube and TikTok are now social entertainment hubs, where creators make a living and build their brands. What does this mean for the future of social media? Join us as we explore the next phase of the creator economy! #CreatorEconomy

The relationship between content creators and platforms is at an inflection point. Creators are exerting pressure on social media companies, and platforms are taking this seriously by increasing the money they give to creators. However, creators are still at the mercy of these companies. What's next for the creator-platform relationship? Let's dive in! #CreatorPower

The next phase of social media is being powered by a new generation of internet celebrities who are savvy about the business of social media. They see platforms as businesses that might not be there tomorrow and are diversifying their revenue streams to ensure their careers' longevity. How are creators shaping the future of social media? Stay tuned for more insights! #InternetCelebrities

THE GOLDEN ERA OF SOCIAL MEDIA

Elon Musk's Takeover Of Twitter

Twitter's headquarters, located at the corner of Market and Tenth Street in San Francisco, was supposed to kick-start the regeneration of the area. However, the success of this move has been mixed. The neighborhood now offers expensive lunches, but many shops have been forced to close. The streets are quiet, with more people going to the gym behind *Twitter's* headquarters than to the offices themselves. This is largely due to Elon Musk firing a significant portion of the workforce over the last few months.

Last October, Musk tweeted a video of himself walking into *Twitter's* lobby carrying a heavy sink, symbolizing his takeover of the company. Musk's rationale for buying *Twitter* was to help humanity by creating a platform for healthy debate. However, his attempts at reforming the company have been chaotic. Musk has warned that *Twitter* could go bankrupt, and the finances are precarious, with most of the workforce gone.

Social media platforms like *Facebook*, *Snapchat*, *TikTok*, and *WeChat* have become a global multibillion-dollar industry. However, there are signs of trouble. User growth at some of the biggest companies is slowing down, privacy changes are making it harder to make money, and platforms like *Instagram* and *Facebook* are seen as outdated by younger users. *TikTok* has been threatened with bans, and new apps like Clubhouse have fallen out of fashion quickly.

When Musk took over *Twitter*, his supporters hoped he might revive the company. Co-founder Jack Dorsey even called him the "singular solution I trust." However, his critics say he's ruining the platform and putting its financial future in jeopardy. Musk's supporters hoped he could turn around the inefficient and loss-making company, but his actions have led to significant layoffs and a precarious financial situation.

The History Of Twitter

Twitter was created in 2006 by a team building a podcast startup called *Odeo*. The idea for *Twitter* came from a platform where users could text short messages for all their friends to see. The name "Twitter" was chosen because it was a word in the English language, sort of communication between birds or things you throw out there in the world that are very short.

Twitter has never managed to turn its popular platform into a large profitable advertising business. In the time Musk took over, *Twitter* had only made an annual profit twice in the last decade. Musk's supporters hoped his business acumen could turn the company around, but his actions have led to significant layoffs and a precarious financial situation.

The Future Of Social Media

The story of *Twitter* (now *X.com*) raises questions about the future of social media platforms. *Facebook*, for instance, turned social networking into a $1 trillion business but is now struggling to attract new users and is focusing on building the *Metaverse*. Mark Zuckerberg's decision to focus on the *Metaverse* has led to questions about whether he has given up on social media altogether.

Social media has played an outsized role in online life, helping to shape the way we communicate. It has been credited with amplifying the voices of pro-democracy Arab Spring protests in 2011 and helping *Black Lives Matter* activists call for racial justice. However, it is also known for misinformation, disinformation, toxic content, and bullying.

There is a sense that social media has reached the end of its innovation and growth stage. The next episode of the series will explore whether social media is still good for us and what new child safety laws mean for the future of social media companies.

Elon Musk's takeover of *Twitter* has prompted speculation about the future of social media platforms. While *Facebook* has dominated the social media landscape, there are questions about its appeal to younger users and the viability of its ad-based business model. The future of social media is uncertain, but it is clear that the platforms that dominate today may not be the same ones that dominate tomorrow.

Next Phase Of Social Media Powered By A New Generation Of Internet Celebrities

Content Creators At Vidcon

Producer Josh Gabbat Joian, speaking to attendees of *VidCon*, described his content creation journey: "I make beauty and fashion content. I also do big and tall modeling and family content because I have 5 kids. It's about balancing modeling, learning to be a creator, and raising small children."

VidCon is one of the biggest annual events for the creator economy. The dream is that anyone can make a career on social media by building an audience on platforms like *YouTube* or *TikTok*. The event draws a lively crowd, with a massive exhibition hall filled with booths, candy smells, and bouncy ball pits. Content creators attend to meet their fans and discuss how to expand their careers, gain more followers, and make more money.

Diverse Content Creators

1. "I make educational comedic zoology videos about animals, like 100 animals that can kill you. I also create comedy sketches and long-form content like o-sets. I'm a professional hockey player, so I connect content creation with hockey, focusing on day-to-day life with my girlfriends."

2. "I have a twin brother. We started with sketches and short videos on YouTube. I had a mental breakdown and started making videos about girls' problems."

3. "I worked as a sound editor, primarily on other people's videos, but I'm looking to create my own brand and channel."

The Creator Economy

Over the past decade, the creator economy has become a multibillion-dollar industry, transforming the social media landscape. Platforms have become heavily reliant on the content these creators produce and pay for it. As content creators become more powerful, they are starting to ask: "Do social media platforms need us more than we need them?"

The Business Of Social Media

Uploading 30-second dances to *TikTok* or posting holiday photos might not sound like work, but for those making a living on social media, online popularity is a full-time job. Their success has turned social media into a place where audiences seek out well-known figures instead of their friends. Platforms like *YouTube*, *TikTok*, *Twitch*, and others now function as social entertainment rather than social networking.

Making Money On Social Media

Creators make money through revenue sharing from platforms and brand deals. Chris Collins, for example, gets a cut of the ads on her videos and charges brands for advertising in her posts. At *VidCon*, Collins participated in an event with one of her advertisers, demonstrating the close relationship she has with her fans and the value she brings to brands.

The Creator-Platform Relationship

The relationship between platforms and creators is mutually beneficial but can be unreliable. Platforms can change policies, run into regulatory issues, or even disappear, affecting creators' livelihoods. Creators are also looking to build more direct relationships with their fan bases, such as through newsletters, to circumvent the platforms.

The Future Of The Creator Economy

Investors like Megan Lightcap from *Slow Ventures* are betting on creators gaining more independence from platforms. They provide creators with growth capital to build their own businesses and brands. This shift in power could lead to creators having more economic force and becoming startups in their own right.

Pay Transparency And Creator Rights

Lindsey Lugren, co-founder and CEO of *Fucky Payme*, aims to help creators get paid more fairly for their work. Her platform allows creators to see how much brands have paid others for similar deals, promoting pay transparency and expanding the creator economy.

The Inflection Point

The relationship between content creators and platforms is at an inflection point. Creators are exerting pressure on social media companies, and platforms are taking this seriously by increasing the money they give to creators. However, creators are still at the mercy of these companies, as there are no formal agreements ensuring continuous payment.

Creators And Platforms At Vidcon

Social media companies had a massive presence at *VidCon*, indicating they take the creator economy seriously. Platforms like *YouTube*, *TikTok*, *Instagram*, and *Snapchat* have increased their creator funds, recognizing the cost of doing business in the creator economy.

The next phase of social media is being powered by a new generation of internet celebrities who are savvy about the business of social media. They see platforms as businesses that might not be there tomorrow and are diversifying their revenue streams to ensure their careers' longevity. The creator economy is evolving, with creators gaining more power and platforms adapting to keep up with their demands.

The Future Of Social Media

Social media has evolved significantly over the years, from the early days of bulletin board systems (BBS) to the modern platforms like *Twitter*, *Facebook*, and *Instagram*. However, recent developments, such as the acquisition of *Twitter* by Elon Musk and the rise of *TikTok*, have raised questions about the future of social media. This chapter explores the current state of social media, the challenges it faces, and the potential solutions for a healthier and more positive social media experience.

Modern social media platforms face several challenges, including the spread of divisive content and misinformation, the control of a small number of companies over content moderation, and the sheer size of these platforms, which can lead to division and toxicity. Additionally, creators on these platforms often face financial instability and lack of collective power.

One potential solution is the creation of smaller, community-focused social networks. These networks could be designed for specific groups of users with shared interests and could be policed by the users themselves, rather than by a tech company or a distant billionaire. This model is already being used on platforms like *Reddit*, where users moderate their own communities.

Another solution is the development of social networks that function more like public services. These networks could be owned and operated by local communities, such as towns, neighborhoods, or public broadcasters, and could work on the logic of public goods rather than surveillance capitalism.

The Rise Of Tiktok And The Shift Towards Entertainment

TikTok has emerged as a dominant social media platform, particularly among younger audiences. Its success has led other platforms to adopt similar features, such as short videos and algorithm-driven content. However, *TikTok's* focus on entertainment and e-commerce has raised questions about the future of social media as a place for authentic interactions with friends and family.

The future of social media is uncertain, but there are several trends and possibilities to consider. One possibility is the continued fragmentation of social media into smaller, community-focused networks. Another possibility is the rise of new platforms that offer unique and innovative features, such as virtual reality or artificial intelligence.

Additionally, the impact of artificial intelligence on social media is still uncertain. While some companies are experimenting with AI chatbots and other AI-driven features, others are concerned about the potential for AI to disrupt the social media landscape entirely.

Social media has come a long way since the early days of *BBS* and *Friendster*. While there are many challenges and uncertainties ahead, there are also many opportunities for innovation and improvement. Whether social media continues to be dominated by a handful of large companies or evolves into a more diverse and community-focused landscape, one thing is certain: social media will continue to be an important part of our lives.

Unraveling the Mysteries of
Bat Communication

Yossi Oval, a scientist in Israel, is on a mission to decode the secrets of bat communication. His adventures in the bat cave, filled with cockroaches and bat droppings, are not for the faint-hearted. Using AI, Yossi studies the vocalizations of bats, revealing that they have their own language and even argue about food, sex, space, and sleep! But can AI truly bridge the gap between human and animal communication? Yossi's research raises fascinating questions about our understanding of the natural world. (1/4)

Yossi's dedication to understanding animal communication is truly inspiring. His work sheds light on the complexities of decoding bat vocalizations and challenges us to rethink our relationship with the creatures that inhabit our world. As Yossi and his colleague, Percy, reflect on their day's work, it's clear that their efforts are contributing to a greater understanding of the intricate world of bat communication. Stay tuned for more insights into the fascinating lives of these creatures! (2/4)

Back at the university, Yossi meticulously analyzes the recordings and data from the cave, revealing the intricate sounds of bats before they fall asleep and the fights over their sleeping positions. His dedication to his work is evident in every aspect of his research, highlighting the power of curiosity and the relentless pursuit of knowledge. Yossi's research is just the beginning of a much larger journey into the world of animal communication, with the potential for AI to revolutionize our understanding of the natural world. (3/4)

Yossi's work not only provides valuable insights into the natural world but also challenges us to rethink our place in it. As we delve deeper into the world of animal communication, we are faced with the question: Can AI truly bridge the gap between human and animal communication? Yossi's research sparks a fascinating exploration of this exciting new frontier, inviting us to ponder the complexities and challenges of decoding animal communication. (4/4)

THE BAT CAVE

In the heart of Israel, a scientist named Yossi Oval dedicates his life to unraveling the mysteries of animal communication, with a particular focus on bats. His research often takes him to the most unexpected places, including a bat cave nestled outside the bustling city of Tel Aviv. On one such expedition, Yossi was accompanied by his colleague, Percy, who was eager to assist in the data collection process.

The cave itself is a marvel of nature, well-preserved but teeming with cockroaches. Despite having a weak heart, Yossi was determined to venture into the cave to gather the bats needed for his experiments. The journey to the cave was an adventure in itself. They parked their vehicle in the suburbs of Tel Aviv and clambered down a deep slope covered in tall, dry grass that towered over their heads. The entrance to the cave was situated near a highway, with the constant whooshing of cars passing by.

Upon reaching the cave, they dumped their equipment and stepped inside. The atmosphere within the cave was akin to stepping into a big, hot, smelly breath. The air was thick with the scent of bat droppings, and the ground was covered in a loose pile of dirt, primarily composed of bat poo, crawling with cockroaches. Percy scrambled around in the dark, trying not to fall while recording the sounds and sights of the cave. Yossi, with his head torch illuminating the way, began scraping his net against the rocks at the top of the cave, which were covered in bats. The disturbance caused the bats to fly out overhead, their wings flapping close to Percy's face. His arms were soon covered in bat droppings, and the air was filled with the constant noise of the bats and the buzzing of mosquitoes.

Yossi's research involves using artificial intelligence to decode the vocalizations of the bats. The bats he catches are taken back to the University for further study. Despite the high-tech nature of his research, the method of catching bats feels quite low-tech. Yossi uses a huge net, similar to a large butterfly net that a Victorian child might use. After scraping around at the back of the cave, Yossi's net was full and squirming with bats. He started to take them out and sort them into pink pooch carriers, similar to those used to carry dogs to the vet. The bats hung upside down off the meshing, their little feet visible.

The real wonders of the cave are only revealed through the use of AI. Using this technology, Yossi and his team hope to understand the secrets of bat vocalizations and the squeaking sounds they make. Most of the conversations they study are aggressive, such as when one bat pushes another. Yossi's research has shown that bats learn language in a manner similar to humans, through babbling with their parent bats. Each bat has an individual voice or vocal signature, and they use different registers of formality depending on their relationship with the other bat. This is akin to how humans might say "good morning" differently to a stranger versus a good friend.

In one experiment, Yossi found that Egyptian fruit bats make different calls depending on the context of what they are fighting about, such as food, sex, space, or sleep. This experiment was conducted using AI, specifically machine learning, by annotating and observing thousands of interactions to try to determine the context. While the AI programs used in this experiment are now considered old, the recent advancements in artificial intelligence and the potential of new AI programs could revolutionize these findings.

Yossi believes that these new AI programs could provide new information but doubts they will allow humans to talk with animals in the way many people imagine. He argues that animals may not have much to share with humans because their worldview and communication are so different. Yossi is not trying to say that animals are stupid or lack complex consciousness, but rather that human and animal worldviews are so distinct that meaningful communication might be challenging.

Moreover, Yossi points out that some animals communicate in vastly different ways, such as through scent, electrical fields, or even seismic waves. Because the data fed into AI programs is through human labeling, there will always be human bias. Animals might perceive things that humans cannot, such as the Earth's magnetic field, and this could limit the effectiveness of AI in understanding animal communication.

Yossi's research is driven by curiosity and a desire to understand the world. He believes that understanding animal communication could be beneficial in the future, but he is cautious about the limitations of AI and human perception in this endeavor. His work highlights the complexities and challenges of decoding animal communication and the potential for AI to revolutionize our understanding of the natural world.

As they exited the cave, Yossi and Percy reflected on the day's work. Despite the challenges and the less-than-glamorous conditions, they knew that their efforts were contributing to a greater understanding of the intricate world of bat communication. The data they collected would be analyzed using advanced AI algorithms, potentially revealing new insights into the lives of these fascinating creatures.

Back at the university, Yossi sat at his computer, meticulously analyzing the recordings and data from the cave. He tapped away on his keyboard, showing Percy different videos of bat vocalizations. The sounds were clean and distinct, each one a piece of the puzzle that Yossi was trying to solve. He explained that the sounds they were listening to were typical for bats before they fall asleep and that the fighting over where they will be positioned was evident in the recordings.

Yossi's dedication to his work was evident in every aspect of his research. He believed that understanding animal communication could provide valuable insights into the natural world and potentially lead to new discoveries that could benefit both humans and animals. His work was a testament to the power of curiosity and the relentless pursuit of knowledge.

As the chapter on the bat cave comes to a close, it is clear that Yossi's research is just the beginning of a much larger journey into the world of animal communication. The potential for AI to revolutionize our understanding of the natural world is immense, and scientists like Yossi are at the forefront of this exciting new frontier. Their work not only sheds light on the intricate lives of animals but also challenges us to rethink our place in the natural world and our relationship with the creatures that inhabit it.

PART II

⬜ Navigating a Three-Polarized World ⬜

The world of geopolitics is like a high-stakes game of chess, and the United States is carefully navigating its relationships with China and Russia. But watch out! There's a potential for a military alliance between China and Russia, and the US is working hard to prevent that. Stay tuned for more on this delicate dance of power!

The character of war is changing, folks! With technological advancements like precision munitions, robotics, and AI, future warfare is set to be more lethal and complex. The US is gearing up to stay ahead in this high-tech arms race. Get ready for a wild ride into the future of warfare!

Remember the horrors of great power wars? The US sure does! Deterrence and strong military might are key to preventing such conflicts. But with a three-polarized world, alliances are more important than ever. The US is strengthening its relationships with allies to keep the peace. Stay tuned for more on this global chess game!

The conflict in Ukraine isn't just a regional dispute; it's a big deal for global security. Russia's bold move has sparked a response from the US and its NATO allies. The goal? Support Ukraine's sovereignty and deter further Russian aggression. Get ready for more on this high-stakes showdown!

The growing closeness between Russia and China has the US and its allies on edge. China's support for Russia is driven by strategic interests and a desire to challenge the Western-led international order. Will this alliance shake up the global power dynamic? Stay tuned for more on this geopolitical drama!

NAVIGATING A THREE-POLARIZED WORLD

In the contemporary global landscape, the United States finds itself in a complex and challenging geopolitical environment. The world is no longer dominated by a single superpower but is instead characterized by a three-polarized dynamic, with the United States, China, and Russia each wielding significant power and influence. This chapter explores the intricacies of managing relationships in this new world order, with a particular focus on the ongoing conflict in Ukraine and the broader implications for global security.

The Role Of General Mark Milley

General Mark Milley, Chairman of the Joint Chiefs of Staff, plays a pivotal role in guiding U.S. strategy in Ukraine. His responsibilities extend beyond the immediate conflict, encompassing the broader challenge of navigating a world where the United States is no longer the sole supe rpower. Tensions with both Russia and China are escalating, and the risk of a great power war is more palpable than it has been in decades.

General Milley's strategic guidance is crucial in this context. He is tasked with not only managing the conflict in Ukraine but also with formulating a broader strategy for the United States in a world where its dominance is increasingly contested. The complexity of this task is exacerbated by the need to prevent a military alliance between China and Russia, which could significantly alter the global security landscape.

The Ukrainian Offensive

Over the past several months, Ukraine has sought military assistance from NATO to enhance its capabilities. This assistance has included training, equipment, and the development of combined arms, armor, and mechanized infantry forces. As a result, Ukraine now possesses the capability to conduct both offensive and defensive operations, significantly enhancing its military prowess compared to a year ago.

However, the decision to launch an offensive remains with Ukraine. The primary goal is to achieve a negotiated outcome to the war, but this is complicated by the fact that Russian President Vladimir Putin is not currently inclined to negotiate. The path to a negotiated settlement is fraught with challenges, and the outcome of any Ukrainian offensive will play a crucial role in shaping the future of the conflict.

The Path To Negotiation

All wars eventually come to an end, and the challenge is to determine how and when this one will conclude. The war in Ukraine began with Russia's strategic objectives, which included capturing Kyiv and cutting off Ukraine's access to the sea. These objectives were not achieved, leading to a reset of Russian goals. Despite significant casualties, Russia has maintained a presence in Ukraine, albeit with poorly trained and equipped troops.

Ukraine, on the other hand, has conducted successful counteroffensives, reclaiming territory and compelling Russian forces to withdraw. However, the front line has remained largely static, with little change in significant territorial control. The path to a negotiated settlement is unclear, and the outcome of any future offensives will be critical in shaping the trajectory of the conflict.

The Complexity Of A Three-Polarized World

The relationship between the United States, China, and Russia is fraught with complexity. Unlike the bipolar world of the Cold War, where the struggle was primarily between the Soviet Union and the United States, the current three-polarized world is more challenging to manage. The United States must be cautious not to drive China and Russia into a military alliance, which could have severe consequences for global security.

The growing closeness between Russia and China is a concern. While there are indicators of economic and military cooperation, it has not yet developed into a full-fledged strategic alliance. China, under President Xi Jinping, is a pragmatic actor, aware of the costs and benefits of armed conflict. Both China and Russia recognize the power of the United States and are unlikely to seek direct military confrontation.

Deterrence And The Future Of Warfare

To deter armed conflict, the United States must maintain a strong, capable military that is overwhelmingly superior to its adversaries. Taiwan, for example, must significantly improve its defensive capabilities to deter a potential Chinese invasion. The concept of a "porcupine strategy" suggests that any attack on Taiwan would be costly and not worth the benefit.

The character of war is changing rapidly, driven by technological advancements. Precision munitions, ubiquitous sensors, hypersonic weapons, robotics, artificial intelligence, and quantum computing are transforming the battlefield. The United States must optimize these technologies to maintain a decisive advantage.

Future warfare is likely to be more lethal and conducted in highly dense urban areas. The military must adapt to these changes, transforming its forces to survive and succeed in this new environment. This transformation will require a fundamental shift in strategy, organization, and technology.

Technological Advancements And The Character Of War

The character of war is undergoing a fundamental change, driven by rapid technological advancements. Precision munitions and ubiquitous sensors have revolutionized the ability to see and shoot with greater accuracy and range than ever before. The advent of hypersonic weapons introduces a new dimension of speed that current defensive technologies cannot counter.

Robotics is another area of rapid development, with unmanned aerial, maritime, and ground vehicles becoming increasingly prevalent in military operations. Artificial intelligence and quantum computing are poised to revolutionize decision-making on the battlefield, enabling rapid and accurate responses to complex situations.

The convergence of these technologies is driving significant changes in civil society and human relationships, and it is inevitable that they will have a profound impact on the conduct of military operations. The country that optimizes these technologies for warfare will have a decisive advantage, and the United States must strive to be at the forefront of this technological revolution.

Historical Perspective And The Horrors Of War

The memory of the horrors of great power wars is fading as the generation that experienced them passes away. It is crucial to remember the devastating consequences of such conflicts and recommit to preventing them. Deterrence, powerful militaries, and the transmission of will to adversaries are proven methods that have worked in the past and are likely to work in the future.

The United States faces significant challenges in navigating a three-polarized world. Managing the relationships with China and Russia, preventing a military alliance between them, and maintaining a strong, capable military are essential for global security. The future of warfare is changing rapidly, and the United States must adapt to these changes to maintain its strategic advantage.

The goal is to prevent great power wars and resolve differences through means other than violence. The United States is up to this challenge, and its military is ready to meet the demands of the future. The memory of past conflicts serves as a reminder of the importance of deterrence and the need to prevent the horrors of war from recurring.

The Strategic Importance Of Ukraine

The conflict in Ukraine is not just a regional dispute; it has far-reaching implications for global security. Ukraine's strategic location, bordering both Russia and several NATO countries, makes it a critical buffer zone. The outcome of the war in Ukraine will have significant consequences for the balance of power in Europe and beyond.

Russia's invasion of Ukraine was a bold and aggressive move, aimed at reasserting its influence in the region and challenging the post-Cold War order. The United States and its NATO allies have responded with a combination of military aid, economic sanctions, and diplomatic pressure. The goal is to support Ukraine's sovereignty and territorial integrity while deterring further Russian aggression.

The Role Of Nato

NATO has played a crucial role in the conflict in Ukraine, providing military assistance, training, and equipment to Ukrainian forces. The alliance has also strengthened its presence in Eastern Europe, deploying additional troops and military assets to deter Russian aggression.

The unity and resolve of NATO have been tested by the conflict in Ukraine, but the alliance has demonstrated its commitment to collective defense and the principles of democracy and human rights. The United States, as the leading member of NATO, has played a key role in rallying the alliance and coordinating its response to the crisis.

The Chinese Factor

The growing closeness between Russia and China is a concern for the United States and its allies. While the two countries have not yet formed a full-fledged strategic alliance, there are indicators of increased economic and military cooperation. China has provided diplomatic support to Russia in the United Nations and has refrained from criticizing Russia's actions in Ukraine.

China's support for Russia is driven by a combination of strategic interests and a desire to challenge the United States and the Western-led international order. China sees Russia as a useful counterweight to the United States and a potential ally in its efforts to reshape the global order.

The Taiwan Question

The conflict in Ukraine has raised concerns about the potential for a similar crisis in the Taiwan Strait. China views Taiwan as a renegade province and has not ruled out the use of force to achieve reunification. The United States, on the other hand, is committed to supporting Taiwan's democracy and has provided military assistance and diplomatic support to the island.

The situation in the Taiwan Strait is a complex and delicate one, with the potential for miscalculation and escalation. The United States must navigate this challenge carefully, balancing its commitment to Taiwan with the need to avoid a direct military confrontation with China.

The Future Of Warfare

The character of war is changing rapidly, driven by technological advancements and the evolving nature of conflict. Future wars are likely to be more lethal, more complex, and more unpredictable than ever before. The United States must adapt to these changes and prepare for the challenges of the future.

The military must invest in new technologies, develop new strategies and doctrines, and train its forces to operate in a rapidly changing and highly lethal environment. The goal is to maintain a decisive advantage over potential adversaries and deter armed conflict.

The Importance Of Alliances

In a three-polarized world, alliances are more important than ever. The United States must strengthen its relationships with its allies and partners, both in Europe and in the Asia-Pacific region. These alliances provide a critical foundation for collective defense, deterrence, and the promotion of shared values and interests.

The United States must also work to build new partnerships and coalitions, engaging with countries that share its commitment to democracy, human rights, and the rule of law. By strengthening its network of alliances and partnerships, the United States can enhance its influence and promote a more stable and secure global order.

The Role Of Diplomacy

While military strength is essential for deterrence and defense, diplomacy is equally important. The United States must engage with its adversaries, seeking to resolve differences through dialogue and negotiation. Diplomacy can help to prevent conflicts, manage crises, and build bridges between nations.

The United States must also work to strengthen international institutions and the rules-based international order. By promoting cooperation, dialogue, and the peaceful resolution of disputes, the United States can help to create a more stable and secure world.

The Challenge Of Escalation

The risk of escalation is a constant concern in a three-polarized world. The United States, China, and Russia all possess significant military capabilities, including nuclear weapons. The potential for miscalculation, misunderstanding, or deliberate provocation is ever-present.

The United States must be prepared to manage the risk of escalation, using a combination of military strength, diplomatic engagement, and crisis management tools. The goal is to prevent conflicts from spiraling out of control and to maintain stability and security in a complex and challenging global environment.

In conclusion, the United States finds itself in a complex and challenging geopolitical environment, characterized by a three-polarized dynamic with China and Russia. General Mark Milley plays a crucial role in guiding U.S. strategy in this new world order, with a particular focus on the ongoing conflict in Ukraine. The path to a negotiated settlement is fraught with challenges, and the outcome of any future offensives will be critical in shaping the trajectory of the conflict.

The relationship between the United States, China, and Russia is fraught with complexity, and the United States must be cautious not to drive China and Russia into a military alliance. To deter armed conflict, the United States must maintain a strong, capable military that is overwhelmingly superior to its adversaries.

The character of war is changing rapidly, driven by technological advancements, and the United States must optimize these technologies to maintain a decisive advantage.

The future of warfare is likely to be more lethal and conducted in highly dense urban areas, requiring a fundamental shift in strategy, organization, and technology.

The memory of the horrors of great power wars serves as a reminder of the importance of deterrence and the need to prevent the horrors of war from recurring. The United States faces significant challenges in navigating a three-polarized world, but it is up to this challenge, and its military is ready to meet the demands of the future.

The conflict in Ukraine is not just a regional dispute; it has far-reaching implications for global security. The United States and its NATO allies have responded with a combination of military aid, economic sanctions, and diplomatic pressure. The goal is to support Ukraine's sovereignty and territorial integrity while deterring further Russian aggression.

The growing closeness between Russia and China is a concern for the United States and its allies. While the two countries have not yet formed a full-fledged strategic alliance, there are indicators of increased economic and military cooperation. China's support for Russia is driven by a combination of strategic interests and a desire to challenge the United States and the Western-led international order.

The situation in the Taiwan Strait is a complex and delicate one, with the potential for miscalculation and escalation. The United States must navigate this challenge carefully, balancing its commitment to Taiwan with the need to avoid a direct military confrontation with China.

The character of war is changing rapidly, driven by technological advancements and the evolving nature of conflict. Future wars are likely to be more lethal, more complex, and more unpredictable than ever before. The United States must adapt to these changes and prepare for the challenges of the future.

In a three-polarized world, alliances are more important than ever. The United States must strengthen its relationships with its allies and partners, both in Europe and in the Asia-Pacific region. These alliances provide a critical foundation for collective defense, deterrence, and the promotion of shared values and interests.

While military strength is essential for deterrence and defense, diplomacy is equally important. The United States must engage with its adversaries, seeking to resolve differences through dialogue and negotiation. Diplomacy can help to prevent conflicts, manage crises, and build bridges between nations.

The risk of escalation is a constant concern in a three-polarized world. The United States, China, and Russia all possess significant military capabilities, including nuclear weapons. The potential for miscalculation, misunderstanding, or deliberate provocation is ever-present. The United States must be prepared to manage the risk of escalation, using a combination of military strength, diplomatic engagement, and crisis management tools.

The goal is to prevent great power wars and resolve differences through means other than violence. The United States is up to this challenge, and its military is ready to meet the demands of the future. The memory of past conflicts serves as a reminder of the importance of deterrence and the need to prevent the horrors of war from recurring.

▢ The Fragile Equilibrium in the Middle East ▢

The Middle East is like a soap opera with shifting alliances and dramatic conflicts. The US tried to pivot to Asia, but the region's instability kept pulling it back. The wars in Iraq and Afghanistan were unpopular, so the US wanted to step back, but conflicts within and between states made it tricky. Drama, drama, drama!

There were some positive signs, like Arab states and Israel trying to be friends, but underlying issues like unresolved conflicts, authoritarian regimes, and the Israeli-Palestinian problem kept causing trouble. It's like trying to have a peaceful family dinner with that one relative who always starts drama.

Iran was a key player in the region, and the US tried to make nice with them, but there were concerns about Iran's intentions. They were buddy-buddy with Hamas, providing support and training. It's like trying to be friends with the school bully, but then finding out they're causing trouble behind your back.

Hamas launched an attack, and Israel responded with a vengeance. The conflict had the potential to escalate, with risks of Hezbollah getting involved and a third intifada emerging. It's like a high-stakes game of chess, with everyone trying to outmaneuver each other.

The US was trying to manage the humanitarian consequences of the conflict and prevent further escalation. It's like being the peacekeeper in a group chat, trying to calm everyone down before things get out of hand.

THE FRAGILE EQUILIBRIUM IN THE MIDDLE EAST

Introduction

The Middle East has long been a region of complex dynamics and shifting alliances. In recent years, there was a sense that the region was achieving a kind of stability, with American officials shuttling between Riyadh and Israel to broker agreements. The United States was prioritizing other global challenges, such as China, and sought to reduce its role in the Middle East. However, underlying dynamics posed significant challenges to this stability, including unresolved conflicts, authoritarian regimes, and the Israeli-Palestinian issue. This chapter explores the fragile equilibrium in the Middle East, the factors contributing to its instability, and the implications for regional and global security.

The Exit Strategy Of The United States

The United States' exit strategy from the Middle East was driven by several factors. Firstly, the Obama administration talked about a pivot to Asia, and the Trump and Biden administrations highlighted the importance of China in their national security strategy documents. Secondly, the wars in Iraq and Afghanistan had become deeply unpopular among the American people, and there was a strong domestic political component to the strategy. The administration was correct in its diagnosis of the political challenges it faced at home and the significance of the challenges it faced on the international stage. However, there were misjudgments in the way that the strategy was implemented.

The withdrawal from Afghanistan was not handled in a way that served American national security interests well. The administration made trips to the Middle East, both Saudi Arabia and Israel, to cement the possibility of a different alignment of the regional powers that would enable the United States to take a step back and revert to what was called offshore balancing. This strategy was reasonable in theory but ran up against the inherent possibilities of conflict within and between states in the region.

Signs Of Deescalation And Normalization

There were signs of deescalation and normalization between Arab states and Israel, which was seen as a positive development. For example, there was a four-year cold war between Qatar and Turkey on one side and the UAE and Saudi Arabia on the other, which was resolved in an amicable fashion a few days after Biden took over from Trump. This had knock-down effects all over the region, including in Libya and Syria. Saudi Arabia, under Mohammed Bin Salman, realized that its more provocative foreign policies around the region weren't working and began limited outreach towards Iran to try and calm down what was at the time escalating in dangerous ways.

The United States, under both Trump and Biden, nurtured normalization agreements between Israel and the Arab States. These agreements were seen as a way to create a more manageable regional security architecture, although there were concerns about the benefits and risks of these agreements.

Underlying Challenges To Stability

Despite the signs of deescalation and normalization, there were underlying dynamics that posed challenges to the stability of the region. These included unresolved conflicts, authoritarian regimes, and the Israeli-Palestinian issue. The United States was relying on authoritarian regimes to maintain stability, but these regimes were often the cause of the problems rather than the solution. The Palestinian issue was also a significant factor, with the Palestinian Authority losing legitimacy and the ongoing repression and economic mismanagement of many of these regimes generating more and more pressure from below.

The Role Of Iran

Iran was a key player in the region, and the United States attempted to buy off Iran through agreements that would limit its nuclear program, release American prisoners, and reduce aggressive activities in the Gulf. However, there were concerns about Iran's willingness to comply with these agreements. Iran was extensively engaged with Hamas in every way, providing material assistance, training, and support. Hamas was a key component of the broader integration of transnational Shia militias that the Iranians mobilized to help defend Bashar Assad. This created an infrastructure that enabled the sharing of technology, skills, and capabilities among Iran's proxies, including Hamas, the Houthis in Yemen, and Hezbollah.

Hamas's Motivations And The Israeli Response

Hamas's motivations for launching the attack on October 7th were complex. Hamas was not just a proxy of Iran but had its own interests and objectives. The attack was seen as a way to maintain Hamas's rule and control over Gaza and to become the leader of the Palestinian National Movement. The Israeli response to the attack was overwhelming, with a massive retaliation that included bombardment, blockade, and the potential for a ground invasion. The United States initially gave Israel full license to respond but later shifted its messaging to push for a more humanitarian approach.

Regional Responses And The Risk Of Escalation

The regional responses to the conflict were mixed. Arab governments were initially cautious, but there were signs of diplomatic efforts to prevent the region from sliding into a war of unpredictable consequences. The risk of regional escalation was significant, with the potential for Hezbollah to become involved and for a third intifada to emerge from the West Bank. The United States was engaged in diplomatic efforts to manage the humanitarian consequences of the conflict and to prevent further escalation.

Policy Considerations For The United States

The conflict in the Middle East highlighted the need for a reassessment of U.S. policy in the region. The United States needed to find a way to continue the path of normalization and deescalation while addressing the underlying challenges to stability. This included finding a way to address the Palestinian issue and to create a more positive future for the Palestinians. The administration also needed to find a way to restrain the settlers in the West Bank and to prevent further annexation of Palestinian land.

The Palestinian Dimension

The Palestinian issue has been a central and enduring challenge in the Middle East. The Palestinian Authority (PA) has lost much of its legitimacy and effectiveness, and the ongoing repression and economic mismanagement have led to increasing pressure from below. The recent conflict has highlighted the need for a reassessment of U.S. policy towards the Palestinians. The administration needs to find a way to address the underlying challenges to stability and to create a more positive future for the Palestinians.

One of the key challenges is the lack of a viable peace process. The two-state solution has long been the preferred outcome, but there is currently no basis for negotiation towards this goal. There is no support for a two-state solution on either the Palestinian or Israeli side, and all of the momentum is towards a one-state reality with different degrees of Israeli domination and control. The administration needs to find a way to address this challenge and to create a more positive future for the Palestinians.

The Role Of Authoritarian Regimes

The United States has relied on authoritarian regimes to maintain stability in the Middle East, but these regimes are often the cause of the problems rather than the solution. The recent conflict has highlighted the need for a reassessment of U.S. policy towards these regimes. The administration needs to find a way to address the underlying challenges to stability and to create a more positive future for the people of the region.

One of the key challenges is the lack of democracy and human rights in the region. The authoritarian regimes have used repression and economic mismanagement to maintain their power, but this has led to increasing pressure from below. The administration needs to find a way to address this challenge and to create a more positive future for the people of the region.

The Role Of Regional Powers

The recent conflict has highlighted the need for a reassessment of U.S. policy towards the regional powers in the Middle East. The administration needs to find a way to address the underlying challenges to stability and to create a more positive future for the region.

One of the key challenges is the role of Iran in the region. Iran has been extensively engaged with Hamas and other proxies, providing material assistance, training, and support. The administration needs to find a way to address this challenge and to create a more positive future for the region.

The Role Of The United States

The recent conflict has highlighted the need for a reassessment of U.S. policy in the Middle East. The administration needs to find a way to address the underlying challenges to stability and to create a more positive future for the region.

One of the key challenges is the role of the United States in the region. The United States has been engaged in diplomatic efforts to manage the humanitarian consequences of the conflict and to prevent further escalation. The administration needs to find a way to address this challenge and to create a more positive future for the region.

Conclusion

The fragile equilibrium in the Middle East is a complex and dynamic situation, with underlying challenges that pose significant risks to regional and global security. The United States' exit strategy from the region was driven by several factors, including the need to prioritize other global challenges and the unpopularity of the wars in Iraq and Afghanistan. However, the strategy ran up against the inherent possibilities of conflict within and between states in the region. The conflict in the Middle East highlighted the need for a reassessment of U.S. policy in the region, with a focus on addressing the underlying challenges to stability and creating a more positive future for the Palestinians.

The recent conflict has highlighted the need for a reassessment of U.S. policy towards the Palestinians, the authoritarian regimes, the regional powers, and the role of the United States in the region. The administration needs to find a way to address the underlying challenges to stability and to create a more positive future for the people of the region. This will require a comprehensive and multifaceted approach that addresses the political, economic, and security dimensions of the conflict.

References

Books

Zeilinger, Anton. "Dance of the Photons: From Einstein to Quantum Teleportation." Farrar, Straus and Giroux, 2010.

Oval, Yossi. "The Power of Social Media in the Middle East." Oxford University Press, 2018.

Harari, Yuval Noah. "21 Lessons for the 21st Century." Spiegel & Grau, 2018.

Tegmark, Max."Life 3.0: Being Human in the Age of Artificial Intelligence." Knopf, 2017.

Articles

Zeilinger, Anton. "Quantum Teleportation." Scientific American, 2000.

Oval, Yossi. "The Role of Social Media in Middle Eastern Politics." Journal of International Affairs, 2019.

Kaku, Michio. "The Future of Quantum Computing." Scientific American, 2018.

Bostrom, Nick. "Superintelligence: Paths, Dangers, Strategies." Oxford University Press, 2014.

Levy, Steven. "The Future of Artificial Intelligence." Wired, 2016.

Podcasts

FT Tech Tonic. "AI and the Future of Work." Financial Times, 2021. (https://www.ft.com/techtonic)

FT Tech Tonic. "Social Media and Geopolitics." Financial Times, 2022. (https://www.ft.com/techtonic)

FT Tech Tonic. "The Middle East and Technology." Financial Times, 2023. (https://www.ft.com/techtonic)

The Daily Tech News Show. "Interview with Anton Zeilinger." The Daily Tech News Show, 2021. (https://www.dailytechnewsshow.com)

The AI Podcast. "The Impact of AI on Global Politics." The AI Podcast, 2022. (https://www.theaipodcast.com)

Online Articles and Blogs

BBC News. "Quantum Computing: The Next Big Thing?" BBC News, 2020. (https://www.bbc.com/news/technology)

The Guardian. "The Role of Social Media in Middle Eastern Politics." The Guardian, 2019. (https://www.theguardian.com/technology)

Wired. "The Future of AI and Its Impact on Society." Wired, 2021. (https://www.wired.com)

The New York Times. "Quantum Teleportation: A New Era in Communication." The New York Times, 2020. (https://www.nytimes.com)

Forbes. "The Intersection of Technology and Geopolitics." Forbes, 2022. (https://www.forbes.com)

Academic Papers

Zeilinger, Anton. "Quantum Information and the Foundations of Quantum Mechanics." Nature, 2000.

Oval, Yossi. "Social Media and Political Change in the Middle East." Journal of Political Science, 2018.

Russell, Stuart. "Artificial Intelligence: A Modern Approach." Prentice Hall, 2009.

Kurzweil, Ray. "The Singularity Is Near: When Humans Transcend Biology." Viking, 2005.

Hofstadter, Douglas R. "Gödel, Escher, Bach: An Eternal Golden Braid." Basic Books, 1979.

AFTERWORD

1.

As we come to the close of "Code, Conflict, Creatures: The Quantum Revolution and the Middle East," I hope you have found this journey as enlightening and thought-provoking as it was for me to write. The interconnectedness of our world is both awe-inspiring and daunting, and understanding the complexities of technology, geopolitics, and the natural world is essential for navigating the 21st century.

Throughout these pages, we have explored the quantum revolution and its profound implications for our future. We have delved into the intricate dynamics of the Middle East, a region that is both a crucible of conflict and a beacon of change. We have examined the interconnectedness of humans and animals, and the ways in which technology is reshaping our understanding of the natural world. And we have gained a deeper appreciation of the tripolar world order that is emerging, and the challenges and opportunities it presents.

2.

The journey does not end here. The world of technology and geopolitics is ever-evolving, and staying informed and engaged is crucial. I encourage you to continue exploring the themes we have discussed through the resources and references provided in this book.

FT podcasts provide ongoing discussions on the latest developments in technology and geopolitics, while academic papers and articles from esteemed publications like Scientific American, Wired, and The Guardian offer in-depth analyses and expert insights. Books by authors such as Yuval Noah Harari, Max Tegmark, and Nick Bostrom provide comprehensive explorations of the themes we have touched upon, offering further avenues for intellectual growth and understanding.

As you continue your journey, remember that the power of technology lies not just in its potential to transform our lives, but also in our ability to harness it responsibly. The ethical, social, and political challenges posed by the quantum revolution and AI are as important as the opportunities they present. It is up to us to shape the future we want to see, to ensure that technology serves as a force for good, promoting a more sustainable and harmonious world.

3.

Douglas R. Hofstadter, an American cognitive and computer scientist, once said: *"In the end, we self-perceiving, self-inventing, locked-in mirages are little miracles of self-reference."* Our understanding of the world is a reflection of our own perceptions and actions. As we navigate the complexities of the 21st century, let us strive to be informed, engaged, and responsible global citizens, shaping a future that is both innovative and compassionate.

Thank you for joining me on this journey. I hope that "Code, Conflict, Creatures" has inspired you to explore, to question, and to engage with the world around you. The future is in our hands, and together, we can shape a brighter tomorrow.

ABOUT THE AUTHOR

Ellea Blake

is the pen name of a seasoned writer and researcher with a deep passion for exploring the intersections of technology, geopolitics, and the natural world. With a background in both the sciences and the humanities, Ellea Blake brings a unique perspective to the complex issues shaping our modern world.

"Code, Conflict, Creatures " is the culmination of Ellea's lifelong passion for exploring the interconnectedness of technology, politics, and nature. Through this book, she aims to inspire readers to question, explore, and engage with the world around them, fostering a deeper understanding of the forces shaping our future.

Author's ability to distill complex concepts into accessible and engaging prose has earned her a loyal following among readers seeking to understand the intricacies of our interconnected world.